The Thoughtful Art of
DISCIPLINE
Teaching responsibility
when your child misbehaves

The Thoughtful Art of
DISCIPLINE

Teaching responsibility when your child misbehaves

Dale R. Olen, Ph.D.

A Life Skills Parenting Book

JODA Communications, Ltd.

Milwaukee, Wisconsin

Editor: Chris Roerden
Design & Layout: Chris Roerden & Associates
Copyright 1994 by Dale R. Olen, Ph.D.
All rights reserved

Published by: JODA Communications, Ltd.
10125 West North Avenue
Milwaukee, WI 53226

PRINTED IN THE UNITED STATES OF AMERICA

Publisher's Cataloging in Publication

Olen, Dale R.
    The thoughtful art of discipline: teaching responsibility
when your child misbehaves / Dale R. Olen.
    p. cm. -- (Life skills parenting series; no. 2)
    Includes bibliographical references and index.
    ISBN 1-56583-014-8

    1. Child rearing. 2. Discipline of children. I. Title. II.
Series.

HQ769.054 1994   649'.64
                                      QB194-224

Table of Contents

Introduction

Teaching Your Child Responsibility

As soon as he could talk, I started correcting him. When Andy spoke in quasi-sentences at the ripe old age of 15 months, they made sense to me. So I figured, if he talked with a degree of clarity, he must be able to understand my words back to him. If he could understand my words, then he could understand what was right and wrong to do, what was appropriate and inappropriate, what was good and bad.

Naturally, I began to tell him what he should and shouldn't be doing. I thought he would get it and then obey. If I told him that it wasn't a good idea to throw his cereal on the floor, I assumed he'd understand and stop throwing cereal on the floor. Of course, that's not exactly how it went. He kept pushing his cereal off his high chair onto the linoleum.

I stayed with it, talking to him, trying to reason with him. Certainly, I thought, he could reason. He could talk, so he must be able to think. If he could think, then he could reason.

No.

Andy didn't work that way. *Children don't work that way.* Just because they talk doesn't mean they think or reason. In fact, they don't reason well until around 15 years of age. Before that time their ability to conceptualize—putting pieces of information into packages that have other similar pieces of information—leaves much to be desired.

Young children learn through their bodies, not through their minds. Action, not talk, makes sense to them.

The more I talked to Andy about keeping his cereal in his bowl and putting it into his mouth, the more he sprayed puffed rice around the kitchen. My words had the impact of a feather blowing against an elephant. Not only did Andy continue to enjoy playing cereal basketball, but he received the added enjoyment of my ongoing contact with him through my barrage of words.

Eventually, I grew frustrated with Andy. He wasn't getting my message. In a moment of weakness (so I thought) I muttered some near obscenity I alone could hear and took away his bowl. He didn't like that much, as I recall. He began to cry, saying "Cereal, cereal."

I'd had it with talking. It didn't work. So I said nothing to Andy and began cleaning up. Shortly he stopped his crying. Five more times over the next two weeks I had to take Andy's cereal bowl away when he threw cereal on the floor. Each time I did so he cried, although he seemed to get over it quickly when I didn't respond with any words but just went about my business.

During the third week, I began to notice that he was keeping most of his cereal in his bowl, or, at least, on his tray. While some fell to the floor (he was only 15 months of age), he wasn't actively throwing cereal as though breakfast were a sporting event.

The lesson, like lightning, knocked me to the floor—well, not literally. *Acting in relation to my child worked a whole lot better than talking.*

That principle has guided my personal parenting of two children, as well as my work in teaching other parents about discipline. Although talking is important—I don't want to deny that in the least—I realize that children under 15 years of age learn best through their *bodies* rather than through their *minds*. In terms of discipline, "Actions speak louder than words."

When your child is born you don't use any discipline for the first seven months. You nurture your child, but you don't correct, reproach or punish her. However, once that helpless little darling develops some strength, gets up on all fours, surveys the room and sees your shiny belt buckle 10 feet away, she's off and running.

Kelly can now locomote. Once she begins creeping, you initiate your role as "Disciplinarian." Your daughter's job is to extend her limits and test how far she can go. Your job is to allow her to push those limits, but to stop her from exceeding them. That's what discipline is for. It puts clear limits in your child's life. That is its only purpose. Any other reason for using discipline doesn't have the best interests of your child at heart.

Sometimes you do discipline for your own interests. For example, you might demand quiet from your child because you have a headache, not because she is exceeding her limits.

Discipline best used, however, has the *child's* interests at heart. It's used to keep your child safe from harm, as in her creeping toward the basement stairs and tumbling down. And it's used to teach your child her own boundaries and the boundaries of others; for example, when she keeps hitting her little brother as though he were a punching bag.

Overall, the fundamental purpose of discipline is to teach children how to act responsibly. In fact, as they get older, you determine their degree of responsibility precisely by their ability to follow rules. If they follow your rules and the rules of the school, the police department and the movie theater, then you decide that your child is responsible.

Approaches to Discipline

Your nine-year-old comes home from school having learned a new and quite colorful vocabulary. He starts spouting three-, four- and five-letter words when you ask him to carry the garbage out to the curb. Bring in a team of parenting experts and ask them how to respond to David's modern use of English and you're going to get a variety of responses.

One expert advises you to use authority and tell David in no uncertain terms to "stop using that language now."

The second authority tells you to change your response to David if—after asking—he still continues using the language.

The third expert tells you to make him experience the consequences of using that language: in this case, the consequence is that communication stops.

And the fourth expert tells you to encourage and command the continued use of that language as part of a "reverse psychology" strategy.

Oh, what to do?

Use any of the four and see what works. All four of these approaches can be helpful at different times.

Depending on the circumstances you can:

1. Use verbal authority.
2. Change the system of interaction between you and your child.
3. Use logical consequences.
4. Use paradoxical responses (or "reverse psychology").

I'm going to spend a chapter with you on each of these approaches. After that I want to look at a few miscellaneous issues important to your efforts at effective discipline.

So, let's get started by first looking at how to discipline using verbal authority.

Chapter 1
Using Verbal Authority

It's eight o'clock at night, time for Karen to get to bed. You say, "Karen, time for bed. Get going." And she goes. Or supper's over and you ask Jason to pick up his dishes and put them in the sink. He does it. You tell Karl to pick up his towels from the bathroom and hang them on the rack. He does so.

Principle 1

Use verbal authority as long as it works.

In the instances above, simply telling your children what to do works. If it works, keep on doing it. You don't need any other form of discipline or power when your words get the job done. It's also much easier for parents to make requests and give commands than to figure out consequences and create elaborate strategies for children to respond responsibly.

Verbal authority is, in fact, the way parents operate anyway. It's the most instinctive, the easiest and least complicated way to get results and teach responsibility. But it works only up to a certain point.

When children start resisting your commands and requests, verbal authority loses effectiveness.

When Karen complains loudly about going to bed at eight o'clock, stalls, futzes around, needs another drink of water and wrestles nightly with the dog, then verbal authority alone won't work. When Jason doesn't put his dishes away and Karl refuses to hang his towels, then verbal authority must give way to other forms of discipline.

Unfortunately, a lot of parents don't realize this principle. They continue to use verbal authority even when it *doesn't* work. They just become more authoritative. They kick it up a notch. They command again: "I told you to get to bed and I mean *now*." The third time, they raise their voice, because obviously Karen didn't hear. Pretty soon they're shouting. Perhaps Karen then goes to bed. The next night the same thing occurs.

Using words in a case like this doesn't work. It

creates distance in the relationship between parent and child; it develops an antagonistic stance between the two; and it leads to prematurely gray hair for the parent (or increased blood pressure).

Yelling doesn't teach children how to act responsibly. Forcing children through anger doesn't move them to value what you value. Cajoling them with a barrage of words doesn't lead to their willingness to cooperate.

Tell your children what you want them to do and what you don't want them to do. If they do it, great. Keep on telling them. If they don't, if they start to resist, and you begin getting angry regularly, then you know it's time to switch to one of the three other discipline approaches.

Please don't keep on talking, commanding and insisting. It doesn't work. You won't teach your children responsibility by verbally beating them up.

Principle 2

With young children, just say "no" and stick to it.

From seven months on, when Timmy begins to creep, get ready to say "no" and mean it.

If Timmy learns early on that "no" means *no,* it helps him set clearer boundaries throughout his life.

If he creeps over to the stairs leading to the basement, say "no" to him and lift him away. Each time he approaches those stairs, you say "no" and take him away. Soon he hears your "no" and stops himself.

As Timmy gets older your "noes" need to be firm and consistent. If he wants to watch another cartoon show and you think he's had enough television, then you need to just say "no."

When he complains, you keep insisting "no." If he cries and whines, you let him cry and whine. But you still say "no."

The first time you say "no" to the cartoon show he may pitch a royal fit. Let him do so. The second time the cartoon show comes up and you say "no" he may still get pretty upset.

But each time you say "no" to the cartoon show, he is learning that your "no" means *no*. Gradually he accepts that and stops pitching his fit when you say "no" to the program.

As Timmy gets older you have to start telling him your reasons behind the "no." But keep your "no" strong and consistent.

Let him have his display of emotion. The purpose of that display is to get you to change your mind. Don't do it. "No" is a vital word in your child's vocabulary. He needs to know what it means. You show him by holding your "no" position despite his protests.

Principle 3

Keep lectures to a bare minimum. Nobody listens beyond the first sentence anyway.

When your children don't follow your instructions you can easily think they didn't hear you or didn't understand. So you lecture.

Not only do you tell your children what to do and not do, but you give them eight reasons why they ought to do what you asked. World peace hinges on their obeying you. Pollution will be reduced if they put their waste in the garbage can. And if they don't follow your instructions, one thing could lead to another, and they could end up in prison, or worse yet, marrying someone who never throws her socks into the hamper.

You lecture to impress your child with the seriousness of his behavior. You want him to have an "Ah-ha" experience, where he says, "Ah, Dad, I understand. From now on, I'll always put my dishes in the sink without you asking me. I never realized how important that was."

Of course, if your son said that—even if he had a conversion experience and meant it—you'd probably respond by saying: "Don't be a smart alec. Just listen and do what I say."

Years ago, a family of five came to see me—three kids, mom and dad. One of the issues that surfaced was Dad's obsession with lectures. Along with spontaneous lectures offered here and there throughout the week, Dad lectured formally every other Saturday morning at a family meeting. These lectures could go on for up to an hour.

The kids were sick of listening. They tuned Dad out as soon as he started. Of course, Dad could sense them tuning out, so he lectured even longer.

If a speaker doesn't think his audience is getting the message, he repeats and repeats it until they get it. So too Dad. Sensing the kids shutting him down, he fueled up to tell them again and again how important it was to pick up their wet towels from the floor.

I asked this family if they'd be willing to try something different. I asked them to go out and buy a number of three-minute egg timers and place them in strategic areas of the house, such as the kitchen, family room, bathroom, at the front door and so on.

Whenever Dad started one of his lectures, the kids or Mom could turn that egg timer over and Dad had three minutes to lecture, and that was it. (Actually, even three minutes is a fairly long lecture. In this household, however, three minutes felt like a microsecond.)

The kids and Mom, too, thought this was a great

idea. Even Dad realized his lectures were not helping matters and was willing to cooperate in this plan.

It worked well. Dad reported much less frustration since giving up the lectures. And the rest of the family was delighted not to have to listen to Dad go on and on. As a result, Dad and Mom learned how to keep their words to a minimum, and to increase their actions in relation to the children. Since Dad couldn't talk for more than three minutes, he had to switch his discipline approach to action. That, he reported, worked much more effectively and efficiently.

Principle 4

On some issues you may have to make requests forever.

You may as well get used to it right away. In certain areas some children will never change. You may have to keep requesting they do this or that until they leave home.

In my house, it's towels. My two teenagers don't know that the long bar sticking out four inches from the wall in the bathroom is for hanging towels. I've tried to tell them about the towel rack. I've showed it to them. I've demonstrated folding a wet towel and hanging it neatly over the rack. As long as I ask them to pick up their wet towels and hang them in the bathroom, they do so. But I want them to perform this simple task without my continued invitation. I want them to hang towels on their own. Yet all my words, threats and punishments have been to no avail.

My son, Andy, has now left home for college. So the problem with him, at least, no longer exists—until he comes home for vacations.

My daughter, Amy, still cannot manage to get her towels from her bedroom into the bathroom. She has made a major improvement, however, which is that she no longer leaves the towels lying in a heap on the floor. She at least drapes them over her closet door. Of course, the door is made of wood, so you can imagine what will happen to the wood in a couple of years.

Anyway, I have become resigned to the wet towel problem. I've lost this battle. I've given up trying to convince my children of the vital importance of consistently hanging their towels in the bathroom. I no longer *expect* them to put their towels where they belong.

I now know they will not do so no matter what. Nothing I have done has altered their behavior.

All that was left for me was to *accept* the reality. My children will not remember to put their wet towels on the rack in the bathroom. Period. Once I accepted this fact, I found my frustration and anger reduced significantly.

Even this morning, when I opened the bathroom

closet door at 5:45 AM to fetch a towel for my shower and found none there, I actually smiled and said to myself: "Dale, this is exactly what you expected. Children will be children."

And I secretly hoped that when my two children marry and have their own children, my grandchildren will leave their wet towels in their bedrooms. Then my kids will know what I feel like now.

I have come to believe that it isn't worth getting upset about or fighting my children over wet towels. The issue is simply not that important. It causes me some moments of personal discomfort, but nothing as bad as Wisconsin weather in January or the kidney stone that decides to descend from my kidney to my bladder.

I accept that my children have left and will leave their towels lying around. On those occasions, I merely ask them to please hang the towels in the bathroom and they do it.

I don't yell and scream; they don't resist and complain. I ask and they do it.

Will they ever do it on their own without my asking? Maybe occasionally, but I don't expect it. I expect that I will always have to ask them, and I will do so.

Until your children grow up and leave home you may have to keep requesting their cooperation in certain areas.

Here are some that come to mind:

- Towels on the floor.
- Jackets not hung in the closet.
- Clothes piled in a heap.
- Winter coats not buttoned up.
- The television left on.
- Going to bed very late at night.
- Acting mean to a brother or sister.
- Never helping around the house without being asked.

These are "normal" behaviors for children. To change, they need constant invitations, and even then they may still not change.

If you expect otherwise, you doom yourself to a life of frustration and anger.

Many children become responsible in some of these areas, but usually not in all.

Be grateful for those things about which your children show responsibility, and accept those areas where they don't. I'd rather my children showed responsibility and initiative in their school work than in picking up wet towels.

Learn to "go with the flow" a little. Realize that you need to keep asking your children to clean their rooms and to quit teasing each other. That's the best you can do with these kinds of issues.

Don't make a major issue out of unimportant things. Use discipline on the major things only.

Principle 5

When you have a need, tell your child about it and request his or her help. But don't use discipline to get *your* need met.

Use discipline when you're trying to keep your child safe or when you're trying to help her become more responsible. Don't use discipline when *you* have a need and are trying to fill it. At least don't use it at first.

For instance, use discipline when your daughter keeps hitting her brother; when she rides her bike into the busy road; when she refuses to go to bed at the appointed hour. As she gets older use discipline when she remains on the phone past a pre-determined time, stays out too late or consistently fails to do homework.

On the other hand, don't start with discipline when you would like the stereo turned down, the board game cleared off the table or the car parked closer to the rear of the garage. These are things that *you* would like. They would make *your* life more pleasant. If your child were an adult friend, you wouldn't demand that he or she turn down the stereo or even take out the garbage. You'd ask politely for your friend to help you with *your* problem.

Try treating your children—especially your older children—as though they were your friends around these sorts of issues. Realize that the problem is yours, not theirs. Respect your children by requesting their help with your problem, rather than lording it over the children by demanding that they follow your prescriptions.

Take the stereo that's blaring (please!). You're sitting in the front room reading the evening paper. Jenny's stereo is pounding out the heaviest of the heavy metal. It's getting to you.

You have two choices: Either you can yell upstairs, "Jenny, turn that darn thing down or I'll take it out of your room and you won't get it for a month," or you can go upstairs and say to her, "Jenny, I'm trying to read downstairs and your music is making it real hard for me to concentrate. Could you please turn your stereo down?"

With the first choice, you're the authority and disciplinarian. You're approaching Jenny from the top down. You're one-up, she's one-down. You're using your power to get your need met, which is to have some peace and quiet. This is not a respectful approach. With no other friend would you demand a certain response, and if it weren't forthcoming would you punish the friend.

In the second approach, you—a human being with

a problem—come to your daughter. *You* have the problem, not Jenny, and you ask her to help you solve your problem. You tell her how you feel and what's happening to you when the stereo is blasting away. You talk about yourself, not about her.

There are a couple of wonderful things about this approach. First, as I said above, you show respect for your child.

Second, you acknowledge the location of the problem accurately. *You* have the problem, not your daughter. Oftentimes in a disciplining, punishing approach, the child feels as though it's her fault, she's bad and no one approves of her.

Third, and most important, you invite the child to come out of her own world and attend to yours. You begin the long process of teaching a child to notice the feelings and the needs of others and respond to those needs. By talking to Jenny about yourself—about your need for quieter music so you can read—you help her understand that there are other people in the world who have thoughts, feelings and needs, too.

Of course, by asking her to turn down her stereo because it's hard for you to read doesn't ensure that it will happen. In fact, she might grumble when you ask and tell you it's not that loud and if she turns it down at all she won't be able to hear it herself.

You ask again and let her know it would help you a lot. Thank you. You leave and she begrudgingly turns it down one small notch. You can't notice the difference. Do you go back yelling and screaming? No. You go back and tell her how you feel when you ask her to help you with your problem and she refuses to do so.

You say: "Jenny, it hurts my feelings a little when I ask you to help me out by turning down your stereo and you choose not to do so. I really would appreciate it if you'd help me out here."

She may still object and tell you it hurts *her* feelings when you don't understand her need to play her music loudly.

Now what do you do? You walk away, letting her know one more time that you'd really like her to turn down the music. And then you let the entire issue go, no matter if she continues to blast her music or turns it down. It may feel to you that you have lost that little battle. I suppose you have. But you are trying to win the entire war.

I don't like this military terminology because it sounds like power again. But I want you to get the idea that you're going for long-range success, which is that your child will learn to become sensitive to your and others' needs.

To continue the example of Jenny and the stereo, let's say she doesn't cooperate with you and keeps her stereo cranked up at high volume. The next time it happens, you go to her again and say: "Jenny, again your music is making it very difficult for me to do my work. Would you please turn it down for my sake?"

If she whines and complains and remains unwilling to turn it down, then you can turn to a disciplining approach.

You say: "Jenny, I've asked you to help me out with my problem around the stereo. You've decided not to help, and I must admit that makes me sad. But since you won't cooperate with me on this issue and it does continue to bother me, something has to be done. So from now on you have a choice.

"Either you keep your stereo on no louder than medium on the dial, or you continue to blast it on high. If you keep it tuned down, respecting my need for quiet, then you are telling me you know how to act responsibly with a stereo and you can continue having it in your room. However, if you don't cooperate and keep playing it at full volume, then it means you don't know how to use a stereo responsibly and I will take it from your room for two weeks. Jenny, it's your choice."

Now you've turned to discipline to get your needs met. But in this case, you are also trying to teach your daughter how to handle audio equipment in a responsible way, being sensitive to other people's needs. If she doesn't get it by your requesting her help, then she must suffer the consequences of not behaving responsibly with her stereo.

If she can't act responsibly with it, she can't use it.

I hope you get the idea of this approach to getting your own needs met. When you have a problem or a need, you present it to your child as *your* problem, not hers. You let her know how her behavior affects you—your feelings and your behavior. Then you ask her to help you solve your problem by doing what you need. If she does so—and most of the time she will if you do this regularly—then all is well. If she doesn't cooperate, you let her know how that makes you feel—usually sad or hurt.

If she still doesn't work with you to solve your problem, then you can turn to discipline in order to teach her that she has to consider other people's needs as well as her own.

This approach works with children from an early age—six or seven—but, of course, needs to be used with teenagers regularly. Any chance you get to let children know how their behavior affects you is helpful. Don't overstate the effects on you, lest you begin to sound like a martyr. Just state how your child's behavior touches your life, and then make a request that he or she change that behavior so your need gets met.

Try it. I think you'll find it helps you get what you need and it keeps the relationship with your child positive and not confrontational.

Talk with your children as best as you can. Issue

commands when kids are little. But also from an early age, let them know what your needs are and make requests of them for help. When verbal commands and requests don't work, then it's time for action.

There are several action approaches you can take with your children in order to teach them how to operate in a responsible manner in our society. Let's look at those now.

Chapter 2

Changing the System

Bruce was eight years old. No way was he going to bed at 8:00 PM. His parents brought Bruce to see me. They looked as though they hadn't slept in weeks. Both of them had drawn faces, bloodshot eyes and an edge of irritability that needed only a tiny shove to dump them into a free-falling display of crazed madness. They pleaded with me to fix Bruce, make him cooperate and go to sleep at night. Eight o'clock was his bedtime. Each night he refused to go to bed and threw a temper tantrum when his parents tried to force him to his room. He'd scream, cry and become belligerent. He'd keep getting out of bed, stomping around the house, waking his four-year-old sister and driving his parents crazy.

The only way he'd go to sleep was if his father

brought in a cot, set it up alongside Bruce's bed and lay on it until Bruce fell asleep. Once Bruce was sleeping, Dad could quietly sneak out of the room and go on with his evening's activities. If Bruce awoke during the night, however, and Dad wasn't there, he would cry loudly until Dad returned to sleep on the cot in Bruce's room.

The parents were desperate and had no idea what to do. So they continued doing the same things over and over. They tried to talk Bruce into going to bed. They yelled, spanked, gave in, slept next to him— over and over again. Nothing changed Bruce's behavior. No matter what they did, the following night Bruce repeated his behavior, oftentimes not falling to sleep until 11 or 12 o'clock.

Bruce and his parents were operating in a *family system*. While Bruce's behavior affected the parents' behavior, so, too, the parents' behavior impacted on Bruce's behavior. A system works as a whole, with all the parts operating together influencing one another. If one gear begins to turn faster, it makes all the other gears turn faster. If one part of the system shuts down, it can cause the entire system to stop.

Human beings operate in systems too. The family is a key system. The way a parent behaves dramatically affects the way the children respond. And the manner in which a child talks to a parent influences a parent's statements to the child.

If Karen sasses her mother, her mother is likely to speak irritably to Karen. If Karen speaks gently with her mom, then Mom can more easily respond with care to Karen. Parents and children have a great impact on each other because the family works as a system.

In the case of Bruce the system looks like this:

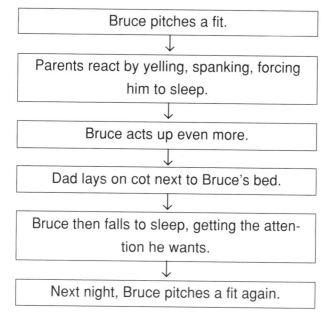

Bruce pitches a fit.

Parents react by yelling, spanking, forcing him to sleep.

Bruce acts up even more.

Dad lays on cot next to Bruce's bed.

Bruce then falls to sleep, getting the attention he wants.

Next night, Bruce pitches a fit again.

The payoff for Bruce's causing a disturbance each night was bushels of attention. When Dad lay down next to him, all the hassle and upset from eight o'clock on became worthwhile. He'd do it all over again tomorrow.

Bruce's "misbehavior" worked.

Principle 6

To break the patterns that don't work, look first to change your behavior as parents.

To stop the awful chain of events from happening every night, I asked the parents to notice the way they were responding to Bruce. The parents realized they were giving Bruce a lot of attention. They knew they had to take that attention away. But how?

Sometimes you have to act dramatically. To change a system at times needs powerful action. These parents were desperate and ready to do anything to stop the misery they were experiencing every night. The most dramatic thing I knew to do was for the parents to *totally* ignore Bruce from eight o'clock on. Pretend, I told them, that he doesn't exist after eight. No matter what he does, act as though it isn't happening.

I failed to tell them, however, to steel themselves for worse behavior from Bruce before his behavior improved. When you change a system, the other parts of the system tend to resist the change and fight it. Kids are the same.

The parents agreed to "give ignoring a try." That didn't sound too convincing to me. When someone says "I'll try it," they usually mean "I'll give this one little effort, but I'm really not at all convinced it's going to work, and I'll probably return to my old approach even though that doesn't work either."

That night as eight o'clock approached, Bruce began his routine—first whining about going to bed, then crying, then creating temper outbursts. When no response came from his parents, he intensified his antics. He screamed, threw things around his room and banged on the walls. Still nothing from his parents. They only turned up the television a little louder.

Bruce then came out of his bedroom and into the living room. He sat directly in front of the television, blocking his parents' view. They said nothing, but picked him up and moved him aside. He presented a running commentary throughout the television program.

Around 10 o'clock Dad and Mom were wearing a little thin. So Mom decided to go grocery shopping at an all-night store and Dad went out to the garage to do some work. Bruce watched television for a while. Then he went out to the garage and tried talking with Dad. Dad refused to notice him.

Around 11:30 Mom came home from the store only to see Bruce waiting for her, sitting on the floor in the garage. When she emerged from the car, he lassoed her around the waist with a rope and tied the other end to himself. (How's that for demanding attention?) At that point Mom wanted to junk this ignoring approach and give Bruce a piece of her mind. But she decided to tough it out.

Around 2:00 AM Dad and Mom went to bed. Bruce was still up, roaming the house. Around four o'clock the parents heard Bruce finally go to bed. At six o'clock the alarm went off. Time for Bruce to get ready for school. Of course he was in no condition to attend school. He felt sick and wanted his mother to call the school and excuse him for the day. Mother wisely told him that it was his problem and he should place the call. He did and announced to the school secretary: "I won't be coming to school today because I had a very rough night last night."

Bruce had to stay in his bed all day. Fortunately Mom had off from work. Of course he slept the morning away. In the afternoon he felt fine, but Mom insisted he was sick and had to remain in bed with the lights out. A little before suppertime he was allowed to get up.

Soon it was 8:00 PM again. The parents readied themselves for another battle with Bruce. They told Bruce it was bedtime and awaited his outbursts. Nothing happened. Bruce went into his room, said good night to his parents and went directly to bed and to sleep.

It worked. And in only one night! Of course, it was quite a night. But by changing their own behavior, the parents were able to change Bruce's bedtime behavior as well. And the new behavior stuck in this case.

Afterward, Bruce continued to go to bed without incident. He had sorely tested his parents' new behavior and discovered that he could not get the payoff he wanted—their attention—by misbehaving.

Because his parents changed their behavior, Bruce learned in one night that throwing tantrums was no longer going to get him the attention he wanted from his parents. So he gave up throwing tantrums.

Principle 7

Once you make a change in your behavior, stick with it no matter how awful your child's behavior gets.

An interesting sidelight to this case has to do with my inexperience as a therapist some 20 years ago. As I said earlier, I failed to warn the parents that Bruce's behavior would get worse once they tried to make a change. He would work hard to get his parents back to their old behavior of yelling and forcing him to bed. He would show them their new responses weren't going to work.

To understand why Bruce's behavior got worse immediately after his parents began ignoring him, you need to know about the basic rat experiments that teach us about rewards and punishments. In those experiments a rat roams around his cage until he accidentally strikes a lever. When he does so a pellet of food drops into a tray. The rat quickly learns that whenever he pushes the lever a food pellet drops down. He continues hitting that lever and every single time he does so a pellet drops. Then one time he hits the lever and no food pellet descends. What does that rat do? He hits the lever again. Nothing. He hits it again. Still nothing. He starts hitting that lever faster and harder. If no food pellets come, no matter how fast and hard he hits that lever, the rat eventually gives up and quits hitting the lever.

On the other hand, if after thirty hits a food pellet drops again, what has the rat learned? He now knows that if you keep hitting the lever, eventually food arrives. His hitting behavior is reinforced more strongly than before.

Bruce was like that rat. He kept hitting the lever (his temper tantrums and acting-out behaviors) and his parents kept dropping food pellets (their yelling, spanking and lying next to him). Once they stopped dropping pellets to Bruce (withheld attention), Bruce began hitting that behavior lever harder and faster. His parents stuck with the program. They didn't drop any more food pellets into his tray, and after one long, harrowing night Bruce quit hitting the tantrum lever.

Once you make a change in the system, expect

your child to resist that change. He or she will try to get you back to the old way by increasing the difficult behavior that you're attempting to change. The child wants you to conclude that your new strategy isn't working. He or she wants you to junk it and return to the old way, which worked so much better for your child.

No, stick to your change. Don't return to your old behavior, because if you do, it reinforces your child's misbehavior. He or she then knows that by keeping the pressure on Dad or Mom, they will break.

Principle 8

Realize that when a child misbehaves regularly, there is a problem in the family system.

Your child's misbehavior is a symptom or a sign that something isn't working well in the entire system. Over the years parents have brought children to see me. Many of these parents have wanted me to "fix" their children, so they cooperate more fully, study more conscientiously and stay within the boundaries of safety. After they describe their child's terrible behavior, my first question is: "And what do *you* do when she does that?" This question surprises some parents. It's almost as though they're saying to me:

"What's that got to do with anything? What difference does it make how I respond? It's my *child* who
is the problem here."

No. Your child is *part* of the problem. The way you
as the parent respond is also part of the problem. Your
behavior, whether positive or negative, shapes your
child's behavior.

For example, your son says, "Good night. See you
in the morning." You say in return, "Good night. See
you in the morning." Your response keeps your son
saying the same thing every night. If you want him to
stop saying that, you change your response. After he
says, "See you in the morning," you say, "No, Jim, I'll
see you at midnight before I go to bed." Eventually
Jim changes his statement to "Good night. See you at
midnight."

Inappropriate behavior works the same way. Becky
yells and screams to get her way. Mom doesn't like
that behavior. She wants it to stop, so she gets angry
with Becky and scolds her. Becky yells more. Mom
follows suit and yells back. Uproar ensues. Mom, in
this case, is as much a part of the "misbehavior" as
Becky is. They both keep the problem alive. Mom's
upset reinforces Becky's yelling behavior. If Becky is
seeking attention, Mom's yelling is giving it to her
dramatically. If Becky wants power, she finds it when
her mother loses control in front of her. Mom and
Becky are locked into a yelling system.

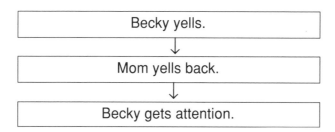

Becky yells.

↓

Mom yells back.

↓

Becky gets attention.

Principle 9

If your responses to your child don't work, then change your responses. Don't keep doing more of the same.

All the parts of this little system are necessary to keep each element operating in the same way. As long as Becky and Mom both respond in their usual ways, Becky's inappropriate behavior continues. Anger, yelling and threats are often the primary responses you turn to when meeting your child's misbehavior. You know that these ways don't change your child's behavior, but you don't know what else to do. So even though yelling back doesn't work, you still use it. At least it lets you vent your frustrations, and you may achieve slight, temporary results. But the pattern continues. The child still yells and screams when she doesn't get her way.

This is solving a problem by *doing more of the*

same. If you tell Josh to come inside for supper and he doesn't, you tell him again and again. You do "more of the same." When he still doesn't come, you become angry and raise your voice. When he doesn't respond you become furious and yell your same command. You're solving this problem by "doing more of the same."

Sometimes this approach works. If you're pounding in a nail and it doesn't go in all the way, you pound harder. You keep doing the same thing, only more so. Eventually the nail goes in. But what if the nail fails to move, no matter how hard you pound? Do you solve the problem by "doing more of the same"? If you keep on pounding, the nail bends and sometimes even breaks. Usually if the nail doesn't go in, you stop pounding and find another approach. Most likely you take the nail out of that spot, move it over and try again. That's using a different strategy.

The same with children. If one approach doesn't work, don't keep "doing more of the same." Change your approach. Do something different. Anything. Just don't keep doing the same thing over and over when it doesn't pay dividends.

To get Josh to come in for supper, Mom first has to look to her own behavior and change that. Remember, change one element in the system and the whole system changes. In this case, instead of calling Josh from the front door, Mom could walk outside to where

Josh is and ask him to come in right now. Just making herself physically closer to Josh might be enough to get him to come in at her first invitation.

Principle 10

**Your child's misbehavior yields positive rewards for him or her.
Know what your child gets from misbehaving.**

What's the payoff for Andrew throwing food around the kitchen? What benefit does Amy derive from whining about bedtime? Why does Michael always say "no" when asked to do something? When you know the answers to these questions you can then figure out how to respond to your children's misbehavior.

If Andrew wants attention and he finds out that by throwing food around he can get it—whether it's positive or negative attention, then he keeps tossing food. When you get stern with him, he gets attention. The attention is more important to him than your sternness. If you want him to stop throwing food, then you must behave in a way that doesn't give Andrew any more attention.

What are the reasons, then, that children misbehave? I ask this question of parents every time I give a talk on discipline and misbehavior. These are the answers I get:

To get attention	Is self-centered
Is fatigued	Is angry about something else
Didn't get her way	Is showing off
To have power	Is frustrated
To defy	Is lazy
To get back	Wants to explore new things

Some misbehavior stops when the reason for misbehaving no longer applies. For instance, when a young child has explored the yard across the street on his own and no longer finds anything there piquing his curiosity, then his "misbehavior"—crossing the street without an adult—stops.

But certain misbehaviors seem to continue with no hope of ending. What motivates these behaviors?

The underlying reason most children misbehave is to gain a sense of *belonging*. Children, like all of us, want to be connected. So they act in any way necessary to accomplish that goal. As many adults comment: "I'd rather get some attention, even negative, than no attention at all."

The most common way to feel you belong is by *getting attention*. Acting out demands attention. When you attempt to stop the "misbehavior," you have to interact with the child. That interaction yields attention. Even if you yell at the child, you are interacting and giving attention.

Especially with young children it's important to realize they don't learn through words but through their bodies. They experience things. They don't think them through to "Ah-ha" conclusions. Kids don't listen to your words. They pay attention to your actions, as I said earlier.

If you go to your five-year-old daughter and say, "Cindy, I love you. You're sweet and special," and you say it quietly and gently, she feels attended to by you. Right? On the other hand, if you go to her and yell, "You get off that table immediately. Haven't I told you a hundred times not to do that? Now you go to your room this minute!" she also feels attended to by you. Right?

In fact, since she's not really listening to your words, but is picking up your emotion and the action of your body, she senses your presence more dramatically in the second instance than in the first. When you yell and scream and jump up and down you are more present to Cindy than when you gently tell her you love her. Your angry expression may actually give her a greater sense of your presence than your gentle expression. That's reinforcing for a child who wants attention. She gets it big time when you're upset and yelling. So she keeps climbing on the table because she gets your attention for it.

Now I'm not saying you should yell at your children rather than gently tell them you love them. Certainly not. In fact, the more you tell them you love them, the better connected they will feel in the long run. The point I want to make here is that by responding negatively and strongly to your children you don't eliminate their attention-seeking behavior. On the contrary, you reinforce it by giving them the very thing they seek—more attention.

In addition to wanting a feeling of belonging, a second reason kids misbehave is for *power.* They grow up in a one-down position in relation to their parents. That's not a comfortable spot to be in, so kids seek the only alternative they know—namely, going one-up. The fight is now on. It's easy for you as a parent to get caught up in the struggle for supremacy. You know your job is to teach, shape and develop this child. To do so you need to be in control. Your authority must not be questioned. You need to win in any conflict with your child. You have to stay one-up.

As soon as your child begins seeking his own one-up position, the fight for power begins. For the child it feels good to win, to get his way and to experience some control in his own world. One of the ways you know you're in a power struggle with your child is by watching the interaction between the two of you.

You get into a disagreement with your son, John. He raises his voice. You raise yours. You both dig in your heels. John challenges your decisions and judgment. The emotional level rises. All of a sudden, John shuts down. He stops arguing. But by this time you're really upset and ranting wildly about your point of view. John is silent and calm, and you're bouncing off walls.

Who has won the power struggle? John has. He's in perfect control of himself, but you're a wild man or woman by now. You're out of control. He's in control. That gives him power. He wins. You lose.

A third reason children misbehave is for *revenge*. If you hurt a child in some way through discipline, that child may try to get back at you.

The most dramatic example of revenge that I ever heard of involved a 12-year-old boy who was grounded for not coming home immediately after school. Early the same evening the parents went out to a school meeting. When they returned home at nine o'clock they found four fire engines at their home putting out a roaring fire engulfing their home. Yes, their son was so upset about being grounded that he decided to get back at them by burning down their home.

In anger, children strike back and often ignore the consequences. They fight back until someone gets hurt, and they often don't care who it is, even if it's themselves.

There's a fourth major reason children misbehave, which parents never identify when they give me their lists of reasons. Children misbehave in order to *demonstrate their sense of inadequacy.* They know what's right and wrong. But they choose the wrong because they believe they are not good or capable kids, and they need to show this belief to others. If Sarah believes she's inadequate, then she acts accordingly. She acts according to her image of herself. And she attempts to get others to see the same image of her. She proves to others that she is, in fact, a failure.

Certainly, Sarah doesn't do this in any conscious way. She's only playing out the beliefs stored deeply within her unconscious mind. She's learned that when something doesn't go well, it's her fault. It didn't go well because she's not adequate.

For instance, she gets a poor grade on a mathematics test. She concludes that she's not any good at math. But her parents tell her she is good at math and has always done well. Their message doesn't fit with her belief, so she demonstrates to her parents the "truth" by continuing to do poorly in math. She doesn't do her math homework, she "forgets" to study for the tests, she doesn't check her work, all in an unconscious effort to demonstrate her inadequacy to her parents.

Children who are forever getting into "trouble" at school often fall into this pattern of showing inadequacy. No matter what the teacher or parents do or say, these children continue to talk out, come late, disrupt the class, get into fights on the playground.

Eventually the teacher and parents get extremely frustrated. None of their efforts have brought about change. They throw up their arms and lament: "What are we to do with this child? He's hopeless."

You know you're getting into this pattern of inadequacy with your child when her behavior keeps getting a reaction from you like this:

"Sarah, I give up. I just don't know what to do with you any more."

That kind of statement tells Sarah that her own sense of inadequacy is now shared by you. In fact, she has now rendered you inadequate as well. You don't know what to do with her. And you're the parent, who is supposed to know everything!

Sarah misbehaves, then, to show you how inadequate she is. And when you shake your head in despair and "give up," you tell her that you too believe she is inadequate.

Principle 11

To change a family system, first try to change your own behavior.

Learn to shock the system. If something is not working, do something different. Shake things up. First, pay attention to what's actually happening. Notice what your child is doing. Then observe how you react and how her sisters or brothers respond. Then watch how your child reacts to your responses. Pay attention to the chain of reactions from start to finish. You will notice that you and the children keep the system going by all continuing to act in the same way.

Whenever Mary gets tired, she picks on her sister, Carla. Carla runs to Mom and complains about Mary. Mom gets upset with Mary, telling her to cut it out. Mary defends herself by saying that Carla started it and Mom always takes Carla's side anyway. Mom gets more upset and tries to defend herself by saying she treats both children equally.

This situation always ends the same way. Mom sends Mary to her room for a "time out." Mary stays angry with Mom. And Carla returns to her play, having won another victory over her older sister.

Mom needs to understand that this whole scene is a sign of Mary being tired. That's the issue that needs attention. She also needs to see that Carla feels one-down to Mary because she's younger, so that when a conflict arises between them, Carla allies herself with a stronger person, Mom. Mom always defends Carla and blames Mary for the problem. Mary feels left out and misunderstood. Mom also feels misunderstood by Mary.

Neither Mary nor Mom like this pattern, but they keep it going by reacting in exactly the same way every time an issue comes up between Mary and Carla.

Once Mom knows what's going on, she can shock the system by reacting differently. The more dramatic she makes the difference the better. In this case, Mom could simply disregard Carla's complaint and take it as a sign that Mary needs some special attention. So instead of "taking Carla's side," Mom goes to Mary, puts her arm around her and says, "Mary I know you're tired. Come over here and sit down with me and let's both rest for a while." Then she turns to Carla and says, "Mary's tired and I'm going to sit with her a bit. You can go back and play your game."

Or Mom might want to sit Carla down on her other side, as long as there is no conversation about the little fight the two girls had.

Mom changed the system here. Whether it works or not is less important than the fact that she inserted a change in the system. Change always shakes up a process. When things resettle, chances are the new system will work better than the old.

Let me give you some examples of ways to shock the system.

- If you're used to shouting when your child misbehaves, make yourself whisper. This changes the entire tone of the interaction. It surprises the child and at least causes her to hesitate, get distracted by your behavior and break the tension that exists. At best, it causes both of you to see how funny whispering seems and to end up laughing with each other instead of unloading anger upon your enemy.

• Get physically lower than your child when talking with him. As the authoritative parent you often stand over your child instructing and lecturing him on how to live. If he resists that, and fights ensue, try standing under him instead. In the musical *The King and I,* the king insisted that all his children and servants never have their heads above his. Every time he lowered his head, anyone around him had to lower their heads more so. It created a great comic scene. Since children tend to feel one-down to parents anyway, it shakes up the system once in a while to talk to your children from a one-down position, at least physically.

• A dramatic physical response is helpful in breaking up the stress and tension between family members. Years ago I was working with a family in therapy. They were trapped in an unworkable pattern of arguing and bickering. Each was so quick verbally that I couldn't get in a word. During the third session they got into a lively argument, with all five family members talking at the same time, accusing, defending, attacking. I tried to get them to stop, but they didn't listen. Eventually, I just sat back and watched them go at it. Still they didn't stop. So, in the midst of their bickering, I slowly fell off my chair.

That stopped them. They were shocked. They looked at me to make sure that I wasn't having a heart attack. When they saw I was okay, they then wondered if they hadn't made a mistake about coming to a weird psychologist. But my behavior stopped their system. I got their attention. I was able to explain how boring their conversation was and how hurtful to each family member.

What if you did something like this at the supper table in the midst of a "yapping match" among your children? Instead of getting caught up in the middle of it trying to get the children to stop, what if you simply fell off your chair, hitting the floor with grace and dignity?

You might be thinking, "That wouldn't stop my children from fighting. They probably wouldn't even notice." I bet they would notice, and I bet such an action would interfere with the argument going on.

- A final example of shocking the system occurred when my daughter, Amy, was five. Amy was a pouter. If she didn't get her way, her bottom lip protruded for miles. She was an expert at lower lip gymnastics. The first couple of times she did it, I thought it was cute. But it soon stopped being cute and became annoying and then downright irritating. I told her to quit doing it, which, of course, she didn't do. I became angry with her then, insisting that she stop that "childish behavior." (She was only five years old.)

Amy and I were getting locked into a system of behavior that caused stress. She wanted something. I'd say "no." She would pout. I would become angry. She would then cry. And I would get even more upset.

The system needed a change. And it happened spontaneously.

I didn't know about "systems" back then, so I didn't plan what I did. I did it by accident, but it worked so well, I've used the approach ever since. One day I said "no" to Amy about something, which today is lost forever in history. She began to pout. For some reason, instead of trying to make her stop her childish behavior, I praised her pouting.

I said, "Amy, that's quite amazing how you can make your lower lip go out so far. I wonder if I can do that as well as you can." So I tried to pout with Amy. I asked her how I was doing, and I asked her for any tips she could give to help me develop my pouting skills. She got into it with me, saying she could pout better than I could. We had a little pouting contest and I declared her the winner—the best pouter in our town. She thought that was funny and we both had a good laugh. I think she even forgot what I had said "no" to.

One moral to this story is: You can't pout well when you're having a good laugh. But the more important moral is: When a way of interacting with your child isn't working, don't keep doing the same thing. Change the way you're responding.

Don't try to force your *child* to change right away. Change *your* response. Your child will change as a result of your change.

Families are systems. All the parts work together to create the way the family behaves. When a child is acting out and consistently misbehaving, that's a sign the *system* needs a change, not just the child.

When your son or daughter predictably misbehaves, look to your own behavior first. What can you do differently? How is your behavior feeding into and reinforcing your child's misbehavior? In what way can you shake up the system rather than the child?

Often, just by shocking the system, you can bring about changes that influence your child's inappropriate behaviors. If such an approach works, great. If it doesn't, then you turn to the methods described in the next chapter and begin the effective work of imposing consequences on the behaviors you want to see changed.

Chapter 3
Discipline by Logical Consequences

First you talk in order to change your child's behavior, as we discussed in Chapter 1. If that doesn't work, then you try to change your responses to the child, as we just talked about in Chapter 2. If that doesn't work and the behavior persists, then you turn to action directed toward your child. This is called "discipline by logical consequences."

One of the first groups to use this approach was the STEP program (Systematic Training for Effective Parenting). Its teachers pointed out that children need to experience the consequences of their actions. If children behave appropriately, they receive the positive results of their actions. If they behave inappropriately, they experience the negative results of their actions. The parents' job is to help their children experience these consequences. Such experiences are worth a hundred times more than an angry lecture about what's right and what's wrong.

Of course, as a parent you also try to protect your child from harm. You don't want him to experience *all* the consequences of his behavior. Some of those consequences are pretty damaging. For example, you don't want your son to experience the consequences of riding his tricycle out into the street. You don't want to have him locked in a body cast in a hospital room while you tell him he suffered the consequences of riding in the street.

So the developers of the STEP program made a distinction between *natural consequences* and *logical consequences*. Natural consequences are those that flow right from the behavior itself. The natural consequence of a young child riding a bike in the street is getting hit by a car. The natural consequence of a toddler sticking metal hair clips in an electrical outlet is a serious shock. The natural consequence of a teenager not studying is poor grades and possible failure in school.

These kinds of natural consequences you want to help your children avoid. So you create *logical consequences*. These are consequences that flow out of the child's misbehavior, but are regulated and controlled by you as the parent. They don't automatically occur, as do natural consequences.

For example, the logical consequence of your young son riding his trike in the street is not being allowed to ride his bike anywhere for three days. The logical consequence of your child sticking hair clips in the electrical outlet is not being allowed to play around that area and having the clips taken away from her. The logical consequence of a teenager not studying is creating a specific time each night for the child to study without the television being on.

At times you can allow natural consequences to take their course. That is sufficient discipline. For instance, if your child is late for school because she didn't get up on time, then the detention she must suffer at school is the natural consequence of her tardiness. You need not add some other punishment.

Many times, however, you don't want your child to experience the natural consequences of events. So your job is to impose logical consequences. You'll see how to do so throughout this chapter.

Principle 12

Think in terms of discipline through logical consequences rather than through punishment.

Some parents think that a logical consequence is the same as punishment. "My child does something wrong, he gets punished," they say. "That's the logical consequence." Or "If my daughter comes home late from school, she gets grounded. If she talks on the telephone past nine o'clock, the phone is gone." What's the difference between punishment and logical consequences?

The difference lies in the attitude and spirit that you, the parent, exhibits. The parent who punishes misbehavior acts as the authority, the one in power who doles out justice. The atmosphere in such a home is one of competition—the power of the master over the irresponsibility of the servants. There results a winner and a loser.

The children in this setting fear the punisher. They try to get around him or her. They lie to avoid the punishment. They play cat and mouse games to see what they can get away with.

Punishing parents see their role as meting out the terms of the crime. They must be vigilant—like police officers—expecting the worst and being ready to pounce when it happens. As soon as their child commits a crime, they swoop in and apply the punishment. "Okay," they say, "that's it. You're grounded for the next month."

Parents who use logical consequences think differently. Certainly they are authorities in the lives of their children, but they don't wield their power haphazardly. They allow their children's behaviors to generate their own effects as much as possible. They see their children as human beings experimenting with ways of living in this world, rather than urchins trying to get away with murder. They respect their children as good people who make mistakes in behavior and judgment at times, rather than evil sociopaths who need to be watched and controlled at all times.

Parents who think in terms of consequences honor their children's decision-making processes, even though those decisions may be harmful or foolish. They prepare their children to face the consequences of their choices, and they simply help to impose the consequences.

The difference between disciplining through punishment and through logical consequences has a lot to do with parents' view of their authority. Punishing parents see their role as one of power. Through power they try to shape and control their child's behavior. Authoritative parents do not give their child *choices*. As the authorities, *they* make the decisions and command the child to follow. If the child doesn't obey, he or she is then punished. Boom, one, two, three. Command, misbehave, punish.

In this approach, children never learn to "think for themselves," a goal most parents want for their children. Authoritative parents try to do all the thinking for the kids. On the other hand, parents who use logical consequences act less authoritatively with their children. They don't view themselves as the major power in the house, whose job it is to make their children right. They see their job as teaching the children how to live responsibly in society. They believe the way to do that is to give children the freedom to make choices and then experience the positive and negative effects of those choices.

These parents actually see a silver lining in children's misbehavior. They know that perhaps the best way a child learns to act responsibly is by suffering the negative effects of his or her poor judgments and decisions. When a child's batteries die because he didn't turn off his game and he can't play it for a week until new batteries can be gotten, he learns that turning off the game is the responsible thing to do. He learns it better by experiencing the week without the game than by Dad or Mom lecturing him about the value of batteries.

Logical-consequence parents see their children's misbehavior as an *opportunity* for teaching responsibility. It's their best opportunity, in fact. These parents are not personally offended by their children's misbehavior. They don't see it as an affront to them. They see it simply as young human beings trying to figure out what works and what doesn't. They see their job as helping their children experience what behaviors get positive results and what behaviors get negative results.

The logical consequences approach is much more accepting of children and much more gentle. However, it is equally as strict and structured as the authoritative approach. It's a results-oriented style whereby parents *walk with* their children and their behavioral experiments, rather than *push* or *pull* them along a predetermined path declared correct by the parents.

Let's get into the logical consequences approach more fully and you'll see what I mean about it being respectful, yet strict and focused.

Four Steps to Discipline through Logical Consequences

The following four elements to discipline give you a formula that will serve you well throughout your years of child-raising. I'd like you to fully understand each of these steps and then burn the entire process into your mind. Each step is important and builds on the one before it. If you leave any step out, you will return to punishing and power as your way of disciplining.

The four steps to effective disciplining are:

1. Give your child the *freedom* to behave appropriately or inappropriately.

2. Decide what your child's choices are and present

them to your child.

3. Identify the logical consequences of each choice and present them to your child.

4. Help your child *experience* the consequences of whatever choice he or she makes.

Some of these steps you most likely do already. Most parents have a sense of consequences. But they present them as "punishments" rather than as "suffering the effects of choices." Let's look at a familiar example where all four steps are applied:

Five-year-old Joan is not eating her supper and instead is goofing around at the table. You give her a choice and you mean it. You have to come to a place in your mind where you can accept equally her eating or not eating her food. Then you give her the choices. You say, "You can either eat your food or not eat your food. It's your choice."

You then determine the consequences flowing out of those two choices. You say, "If you eat your food, then you can have dessert. If you don't eat your food, you cannot have any dessert. It is your choice." That's it. No more talking. No more nagging about eating all her food. When dessert time comes, you help Joan experience the consequences of *her* choice. If she has eaten her food, you give her the dessert. If she hasn't eaten her food, you withhold dessert, much to Joan's chagrin.

You allow Joan to choose a behavior. When she

does so, she also chooses the consequences of that behavior. You, as the parent, set up the choices and the consequences of each choice. After Joan makes her decision, you help her experience fully the consequences of that decision. Anger, upset, lots of talk, arguing and punishment are no longer needed as part of your way of teaching your child to act more responsibly.

Principle 13

Give your child the freedom to behave improperly as well as to behave properly.

You heard that correctly. In order to discipline effectively, which means without anger, you need to give your child the freedom to misbehave. In fact, your son or daughter already has that freedom. No matter what your rules are, your child can choose to disobey them. And most children do disobey some of the rules of their parents.

If you want to teach your child how to act *responsibly*, you need to allow him or her to make the choice of acting *irresponsibly*. By doing so, your child experiences the negative consequences of such behavior, and learns that it doesn't work well to continue that behavior.

For children to function in an independently responsible manner, they need some freedom to make
their own decisions. The kinds of choices children
need to exercise are not simply picking the flavor of
ice cream they want or the color shirt they prefer.
They need the fundamental choice to behave appropriately or inappropriately in the family, school and
societal systems. Essentially, you need to give your
children permission to choose whatever behavior
they desire. Then your job is to help them experience
the consequences of the choices they make.

By granting such permission, two results occur:

1. Your children get the opportunity to practice
   decision-making skills for responsible behavior; and

2. You discipline without anger.

Yes, you can discipline without anger, but only
when you believe your children have the choice to
misbehave. In fact, they *will* misbehave. It's in the
nature of kids to do so. They have to test the limits,
explore the possibilities and learn for themselves
what works and doesn't work. You won't be surprised
when they make poor decisions. You expect it. You
can then let go of your inner *demand* that your
children always follow the true and tried way of
living—your way.

When they choose not to follow your rules and
subsequently make mistakes in judgment, then you

can enter the scene in order to help them experience the consequences of their choices. But because you know that they at times will make mistakes, and because you are not internally demanding that they always must be perfect, you can approach the disciplining process without anger.

Try to capture the spirit of giving your children choices and meaning it. If you say to your daughter, "Jessica, you can eat your broccoli or not, it's your choice," then mean it. Don't secretly be insisting that she'd better eat that food. Often, parents say the words that suggest freedom of choice, but they don't mean it. I overheard a mother asking her son if he wanted some corn. When he said no, she replied, "Well, I think some would be good for you," and proceeded to give it to him anyway. That's not giving the child choice.

It's hard for parents to actually give choice to children. When my father was in his seventies and I was 40 he still found it hard, at times, to give me the freedom to choose. One birthday I was visiting my parents while they were staying for the winter in Jekyll Island, Georgia. Customarily on birthdays my parents would give each of us a card with a check in it. My dad handed me the card and said to read the note inside. The note said:

Happy birthday, Dale. We didn't enclose a check because we're away from home. Would

you like a check now or do you want to wait until
Mom and I return home next month?

Love, Dad and Mom

My dad returned from the kitchen and asked what
I'd like. I said I'd take the gift check now. Without
missing a breath my dad responded, "No, I think it
would be best to wait until we get back to Milwaukee." So much for my being a 40-year-old responsible
adult. My dad was afraid I'd lose the check while
traveling. He didn't really give me a choice. He was
still acting as my parent, trying to protect me from all
harm.

So let go of your need to have the children always
follow your way. Even though you know your way is
best, they have to learn that truth through the consequences of their behavior, rather than through your
insistence that you are right.

Principle 14

**Perform each step of the discipline
process consistently.**

Nine-year-old Joey often nags, whines and cries
when he doesn't get his way. His parents want such
behavior to stop, and they would like Joey to learn
more responsible behavior. How can they get him to
do so using the logical consequences approach?

Steps in stopping Joey's whining

1. Parents give Joey the *choice* to behave or misbe-have.	They say: "Joey, it's your choice."
2. Parents determine what the possible choices are.	They say: "Either you talk calmly and reasonably or you continue whining and nagging."
3. Parents determine the logical conse-quences for each choice.	The consequence of calm and reason-able talk is that the parents can more easily receive the child's message and communicate with the child. In other words, communication takes place when both parties are presenting themselves rationally and sensibly. The consequence of whining and nagging and crying is that the parents find it very difficult to receive such messages and oftentimes become irritable in return. As long as Joey keeps up the nagging he is incapable of receiv-ing any messages from his parents. Thus, the real consequence of Joey's behavior is a breakdown in communica-

	tion. When communication has broken down, parents and Joey are wasting time with each other and should simply stop dealing with the other at that moment. So, the parents say: "Joey, if you talk calmly and reasonably now, I'm happy to continue our conversation. If you continue whining and nagging, I simply will not communicate with you at this time. It's your choice."
4. Parents help child experience the consequences of his choice.	If Joey stops whining and talks reasonably, the parents continue a dialogue with him. If Joey whines on, the parents totally ignore Joey and go on with whatever they are doing.

Each step along the way is important. Don't jump past any of them.

Step 1

You give your child the *choice* to behave appropriately or inappropriately.

As I've said, your attitude is critical to effectively discipline through the use of consequences. If you can recognize that your daughter's misbehavior serves an important function in her growing up, then you can more effectively work with her actions. Her misbehavior offers the best opportunity to teach her how to make more responsible choices.

Step 2

You determine what the possible choices are.

You, the authority, operate here. You present the limits within which your children can decide. Usually the choices are an "either-or" type:

"Either you do this or you don't do this."

"Either cut the grass or don't cut the grass."

"Either take a bath or don't take a bath."

Most of the time you will present directly opposite choices to your children. And generally those two choices arise spontaneously in you. Occasionally you need to exclude specific possibilities that you feel are harmful to your children.

"Either you can go to the ball game with the guys or you can stay home."

You have excluded as a possibility the party at Frank's house while his parents are out of town. As the parent with authority, you can exclude those choices that are not in your children's best interests. Now you are ready to take on the consequences of your children's choices.

Steps 3 and 4

You determine the logical consequences for each choice and help your children *experience*

those consequences.

Here comes the creative part of parenting—trying to discover the logical consequences of your children's behavior. What is the consequence of your four-year-old daughter playing with things on your desk while you are working? You ask her not to fool around in the den and to leave until you complete your work. She doesn't respond to your request. So you set up the choices for her and the consequences:

"Jill, either you leave the den until I'm finished or you don't. If you leave, I'll swing you on the swing when I'm finished. If you don't leave right now, I'll take you to your room where you will stay until I do finish. It's your choice."

You then hope she leaves without a complaint or a tear.

If you use this approach, be sure you actually finish your work and reward your child's cooperation by playing with her.

Sometimes parents don't carry through on their promises. They don't ever get finished with their work. Then, your child learns that her patience doesn't bring about what you promised. The message she learns instead is "that by being patient and cooperative I lose out." The consequence of trusting your word is *getting ignored*.

So make sure that when you set up consequences you carry out your end of the arrangement.

Thinking up the consequences of misbehavior can be pleasant entertainment when done with other parents. Let's look at typical "misbehaviors" and what the consequences might be:

Behavior	Indicates	Consequences
Temper tantrums	Inability to communicate effectively	Communication breaks down, so you ignore child's yelling and cease talking in return.
Children fighting	Inability to be together	You separate them to opposite corners of the house where they sit in isolation.
Little child riding bike in road	Unawareness of danger and possible harm, as well as irresponsible use of bike	A physical pain is created by spanking rather than by collision with a car; or the bike is taken away for a time; or the child is brought into the house for a period of time.
Getting up in time for school	Inability to handle time in a responsible way	For every minute the child remains in bed in the morning, she must go to bed three minutes earlier in the evening. Or (if feasible) let her miss the school bus and don't take her by car.

Behavior	Indicates	Consequences
Not doing home-work	Poor use of time for important needs	Determine how much time your child would spend on homework; then, each afternoon, he spends that time sitting at the table, whether he does anything or not, until he shows responsible action regarding homework.
Spilling things at table	Irresponsible use of food and dishes and/or simply an accident	A mess is created. You instruct your child to clean it up. If it was an accident, you may help your child. If it was an irresponsible act, you might send your child away from the table.
Young child getting into things while you are on the phone	An awareness that he can "get away with murder" at that time and have the freedom to misbehave	Whenever you are on the phone in the future, your child must immediately go to the corner chair and sit there until the phone conversation is over.

Behavior	Indicates	Consequences
Stealing in the house	Lack of respect for others' belongings	Your child must return what was taken; or you may take from the child, with his or her knowledge, some valued possession for a period of time.
Staying out past curfew or going out without your knowing the destination	Lack of responsibility in dealing with freedom in the social arena	The child is grounded.
Children not doing expected chores around the house	Unwillingness to cooperate in the normal functioning of the house	You can do their chores and charge them for services just as a maid would be paid to do them.

In the examples above, the consequences are intended to stimulate your thinking. The best consequences must be created directly out of the situation and according to the child's interests and needs.

Sending your child to her room if it's stashed with television, stereo, telephone and Nintendo is not an effective consequence for her fighting with her brother. You know your child well enough to know what consequence will cause her some pain. Consequences for inappropriate behavior need to create a hardship for your child. A consequence needs to be experienced by your child as more negative than the behavior that led to it.

Principle 15

Consequences must flow directly out of the child's misbehavior and cause hardship for your child.

Let's look more fully at the situation in which your child doesn't do his chores around the house (final example on page 75). When Paul doesn't carry out the work he's assigned, the consequence is that you do the chores and charge him money for your services. This logical consequence works only for an older child who places some value on money. It also assumes that the child has some source of income, such as allowances, babysitting or paper route money.

Let's say the chore is taking out the garbage every night. Paul, who is 13, always needs reminding. If his parents don't keep after him each day, he "forgets." Dad and Mom do certain chores around the house, sister Beth does some chores, and Paul is supposed to do some, too. If they all assume their responsibilities, the household runs efficiently.

But what would happen if Dad and Mom stopped cooking, cleaning and changing the oil in the car? The work wouldn't get done, and other people would have to be hired to perform these tasks. In other words, the work that Dad and Mom don't do would have to be purchased.

The same applies to Paul. If he doesn't do his tasks, the consequence is not an irate parent, but Paul paying for services he *chooses* (there's that word again) not to perform. So if Paul chooses to not take out the garbage at the appropriate time, Dad or Mom do it and charge Paul for their service. The fee for the chore is determined in advance by the parents, based on the amount of income Paul brings in. They make the fee stiff enough so Paul feels the negative effect and decides it is better for him to take out the garbage rather than lose his spending money.

In presenting this arrangement the parent might say: "Paul, either you take the garbage out or you don't take it out. If you take it out, you will be helping us and creating a cooperative and happy atmosphere in the house. If you don't take it out, I will do it for you as a service. But I expect to be paid for that service, just as I would have to pay a maid or a cook to do my chores if I decided not to do them. So each time I take out the garbage for you, I will charge you fifty cents. It's your choice."

The parents might also indicate that the garbage is to be taken out by a certain time, and that they will remind Paul only once. This strategy has been most effective in helping parents help their children act more responsibly toward household tasks.

An observation about allowances. I do not believe that the granting of an allowance should be tied to children doing or not doing jobs around the house. I believe that some spending money is simply a part of life today, and that children should have some money in their pockets. The granting of an allowance, then, is not held over children to get them to perform. It is simply there as part of this family's life.

However, if Paul refuses to pay his bill, then you can "garnishee" his allowance. The next week you pay him only fifty cents instead of his usual two dollars because you took out the garbage three times.

Principle 16

Stick to your consequences once you set them.

Perhaps the major pitfall in attempting to teach responsibility through logical consequences has to do with consistency and discouragement. Because the children want you to go back to the way you were responding before, they give you the impression that your new approach doesn't faze them. When Mom explains to Paul that she will be charging for her services, Paul responds: "Great! Then you'll be my servant and I'll pay you. No problem."

Do not become discouraged by that response. And do not change your response. Accept your child's statement and then carry out the consequences as you set them up. And *continue* to carry out the consequences. Don't revert to your old pattern of responding simply because your logical consequence "didn't work" right away. Stay with your strategy for at least three weeks. Then if the desired results have not yet been achieved, keep the same consequences and *add* to them. However, if you revert to your former style of responding, your child wins the game and you remain as frustrated as before.

If the consequence you impose doesn't seem to work, you may have selected a consequence that is reinforcing the inappropriate behavior and is not experienced as a hardship by your child. In that case, you can change the consequence.

But hang in there. Your child's behavior may get worse before it gets better. Stick to the consequences you set up. If you stay consistent and firm, your child's behavior and sense of responsibility should improve.

Principle 17

Be selective about when to use consequences with your children. Don't overdo it.

Choose your battlegrounds carefully. Don't bring out the big cannons for tiny issues. And don't attempt to set consequences for every piece of your child's behavior. To start with, try this approach on only one behavior you'd like to see changed. Don't get too enthusiastic and attempt to place a consequence on every little action your child takes that annoys you.

Decide which situation you want to discipline— because talking hasn't worked—and then think clearly about what consequences you can impose. Wait for the next time your child does the deed. Then, instead of punishing him immediately, sit him down and set out the choices and the consequences. Use this occurrence as the opportunity to establish the choices he has and the consequences that flow out of those choices. Say:

"Karl, when you're done watching television, you either can leave your dishes in the family room or you can bring them into the kitchen and put them in the sink. If you leave your dishes in the family room, it tells me you don't know how to be responsible in that room, so you won't be able to go in the family room for three days. If you choose to bring your dishes into the kitchen, then it tells me you are responsible in the family room and you can continue using it and the television. It's your choice."

Then you wait. The next time Karl forgets to bring his dishes into the kitchen, you quietly tell him he has chosen not to be in the family room for the next three days. And you enforce that consequence. You don't give any lecture. Just present the consequence.

If he leaves his dishes in the family room a week later, you enforce the same consequence. No arguing or yelling, just impose the consequence.

Once Karl's behavior becomes acceptable, you can move on to other behaviors if you have a list. Just don't throw a hundred consequences at your child at once. It's too hard for you and your child to keep track of it all.

I have talked with parents who have decided on certain consequences for certain behaviors and have formed a contract with their children. They identify five or six situations and explain to the children the consequences of each choice they make. It's like setting up the rules of the game before the action begins. A contract is often helpful in families because it makes things clear. Of course, there are always new situations not covered by the original contract. These things must be dealt with on the spot.

Using logical consequences is the best approach to discipline that I know—once talking with your child has failed. This approach allows you to help your child *experience* the effects of his or her activity without you having to lecture, get upset and hurt your relationship with your child.

Sometimes using consequences doesn't work, though, no matter how consistent you are, how creative in thinking up logical consequences, or how painful the consequence is to your child. This is especially true when you have an "oppositional child." In this case you need another approach—paradoxical parenting. That's what the next chapter is about.

Chapter 4
Discipline Through Paradox

Parenting experts have a new term for an old reality. When you and I were kids this approach was called "reverse psychology."

Today we call it "paradoxical parenting." It has a nice ring to it, wouldn't you say?

You use paradox when your child opposes you at every turn, as in when you say black, he says white. You use paradox when the first word out of your child's mouth is "no."

Kids show opposition as a way of getting attention. They certainly get yours when they oppose you. They can often hook you into a major fight, keeping you emotionally present for a long and intense time.

They also oppose you in order to take power in the relationship. Being one-up to a parent is quite a reward for children. When you engage them in the power struggle, they already win, because the struggle itself is so stimulating for them. They watch you get upset and lose emotional control while they remain relatively calm and in control. That's their victory, and they will come back again and again to beat you at the game of power.

Furthermore, children don't know when to quit the power game. They play it until someone gets hurt, whether that be you or them.

As the smarter person here, you need to get out of power games with your children so they or you don't get beaten up too badly. Using a paradoxical approach is one way out of the power struggles you face with your children.

Finally, your children can oppose you in order to separate from you, which they should do anyway from their preteen years on. Unfortunately, opposition is one of the more distressing ways some children move to separate from you.

Children who are oppositional continue doing things after you ask or command them to stop. They keep using foul language even though you have begged them not to. They throw temper tantrums when they don't get their way. They argue and try to negotiate every point of every decision made against them. They keep their rooms messy no matter what you do to insist on neatness.

A word of caution here. All children oppose their

parents at some point. That doesn't mean they are "oppositional children." Your children may be oppositional only in one or two areas. That's normal. You can use paradox with them in those areas.

Other, more difficult children, are oppositional in most areas. These children need paradoxical approaches as well. But they may well need more than that. They may also need counseling.

Or their parents may need counseling because the opposition showing up in the children may be a result of the way the parents are relating with and responding to the children.

When you try to use power against children who are opposing you, you set up force against force. The social psychological principle that applies here is this:

The greater the force exerted, the greater the resistance to the force. The more pressure you apply to your child, the more your child will press back. When both of you press hard against each other, you can be assured one or both of you will get hurt.

It's quite natural to push back when you get pushed. Even as an adult, if someone tells you that you can't do something, you are likely to go ahead and do it. You resist force, especially when it seems excessive. And to children, most parental authority seems excessive. So they resist it. If you resist back, then you have a power struggle on your hands.

Principle 18

Create a double bind situation for your child.

When you discipline through paradox, you set up a double bind for your child that not only causes discomfort for him but also a winning situation for you. Since Tommy is oppositional—he says "blue" whenever you say "yellow"—his payoff is to go against whatever you say. That gets you upset. You engage Tommy and he wins your attention and you lose your peace of mind.

In paradoxical parenting, you go *with* Tommy instead of *against* him, thus throwing him off balance.

For example, Tommy swears a lot and doesn't stop when you request it. The paradoxical approach says that you tell him to continue to swear. You *want* him to swear. In fact, you insist that he swear.

Now here's the double bind: If Tommy is oppositional and you command him to do what he is already doing, he will want to do the opposite; namely, to stop swearing. So if he stops swearing, he is still acting in an oppositional way, but you have gotten what you wanted—his swearing behavior to stop. If he chooses to continue swearing, he is no longer oppositional, because he is doing what you commanded him to do.

By following your command to continue swearing, he can't get into a power struggle with you. He can't get additional attention from you. He can't get you upset. So, either way you win. But more important, Tommy is confused. And in his confusion, he is forced to respond differently. You have shaken up his system of rewards and gratification.

Steps in Using Paradox

You need to follow four steps in using paradox effectively. Those steps are:

1. Go *with* the behavior instead of against it.
2. Reframe and respect your child's behavior.
3. Command the very behavior you want to stop.
4. When appropriate, predict a relapse in the changed behavior.

I want to go through each step with you.

Principle 19

Go *with* your child's behavior instead of against it.

In jujitsu, when an enemy throws a punch, you go with the flow of the punch rather than oppose it by walking into it. By going with the direction of the punch, it is much less painful and it throws the puncher off balance because he is lunging at you. In his off-balance position, you can grab him by the arm and easily throw him to the floor. Let's not get carried away here with the analogy to discipline with our children. But the off-balance aspect of jujitsu is important. By going with your child's resistance instead of against it, you throw him off balance and thereby change the dynamics of his and your own behavior. Now you have a better chance of relating in a new and more positive way.

By not opposing your child's behavior, you aren't supporting or approving it. You are simply acknowledging it as being there, and there for a good reason. You might not know what that reason is, but you can know there is "method to this madness." By going with the behavior, you become more accepting of it as part of your child's development and you become more accepting of reality as it is and not as you insist it must be.

Principle 20

Reframe and respect the experience of your child.

Tammy's room remains a mess no matter how often you plead, beg and command her to clean it up. You decide to use paradox to deal with this thorn in your side. You are going to go with the messy room instead of against it. You accept the reality of the "disaster area." Now you have to reframe your child's experience of the dirty room. Reframing means seeing it in a different way. You have to first change your view of that room and then present the reframed view to your daughter.

How can you view this "junkyard" differently? Well, you can see Tammy's "non-effort" to keep her room clean as a "creative effort" to decorate in a unique and distinctive fashion. You can see the mess as "artistic expression of individuality." You can see it as a "bold statement against the rigid thinking of rules, boundaries and laws that inhibit the free child within."

Do you get the idea? You can actually have fun with these types of situations. Sit with your friends and try figuring out new meanings of your daughter's messy room. Sure, some of these interpretations are done tongue in cheek, but they do help you reframe the situation.

Reframing helps you because you learn to let go of your insistence that reality be according to your ideal. Other people, including your children, dance to a different beat than you do. Try to add different spins to your daughter's messy room. And know that in her mind, she sees her messy room as a positive, not a negative. She likes it that way. It doesn't bother her.

Respect her view of the room, what it means to her

and why she decorates the way she does. You may not like it, but you can respect the fact that she is expressing something about herself through what you perceive as a mess.

Present your reframed view to your daughter. You can say: "Tammy, it must be important for you to keep your room as it is. In some way, beyond my comprehension, your room expresses you and what you believe in. I want to encourage that expression." We'll get to the rest of your statement to her in the next step of the process. For now, though, realize that you first want to go *with* your daughter's behavior rather than against it. And secondly, you want to interpret her behavior as something that is positive and helpful to her, even though to you it is annoying and negative.

Principle 21

Command the behavior you wish to stop.

This is the heart of paradoxical parenting. You tell your child to do exactly what it is he or she is doing, even though that's the behavior you want stopped. You don't just *suggest* the behavior, you *command* it. You insist that your child continue the behavior being presented. By doing so you force your child to stay oppositional, which ends the inappropriate behavior; or to cooperate with your order and keep doing the disturbing behavior.

In the example of Tammy's messy room, you say: "I know it's important for you to keep your room this way. In fact, there must be some significant good in your doing this. So I want you to continue messing up your room. In fact, I insist that you keep your room a mess." That's the paradoxical approach.

As you can imagine, this approach works best with younger children. Teenagers can usually see through it, especially in the case of the messy room. They might recognize the reverse psychology and continue keeping their room messy. Younger children won't recognize the strategy here, and if they are truly oppositional, they may actually start cleaning their rooms.

In this example, you can combine this paradoxical approach with the logical consequences approach. After telling Tammy you insist that she keep her room a mess, you can inform her that you will help her do so by throwing other things in her room as well. Use her room as a storage area. Put old clothes in there, heaping them on the floor by her bed. Put boxes of old files, unused camping equipment, out-of-date books and luggage in her room. Help her keep her room a mess. That way she experiences the consequences of her behavior.

Let's look at a couple of other examples of using paradox to stop oppositional behavior. Earlier I mentioned Tommy's using foul language. He won't stop no matter how often you ask him to. So you use paradox. You say:

"Tommy, somehow swearing must be important for you to do. It seems as though it's a strong way for you to express your feelings and thoughts. So I want you to sit here in this chair and for the next 15 minutes use as much foul language as you possibly can. I insist that you do this because it seems as though it's good for you to get all those thoughts and feelings out."

You are going *with* Tommy's behavior, reframing it as something useful in expressing feelings, and you are commanding him to do the very behavior you wish stopped. He may say to you: "Mom, that's really dumb. I'm not going to do that." Then he remains oppositional, but he stops swearing. Or he may sit there and cooperate with you and begin swearing. But he will stop before 15 minutes are up because it's too hard for most children to swear for 15 minutes straight.

You might be saying, "Not my child. He could sit there for an hour and swear." Probably not. If Tommy sits there and swears for 15 minutes, then you say to him:

"Tommy, you must have so much feeling and so many words in you, I want you to spend another 10 minutes expressing yourself even more. That wasn't as expressive as I know you can be. Give it your best shot."

You see what's happening here? By going *with* Tommy instead of *against* him, you are taking away his reward, namely the conflict he can generate between him and you. You have effectively changed the dynamic of your interaction, and that's the important aspect of paradoxical parenting.

Closely related to the example above is the common problem of a young child throwing a temper tantrum. Whenever her mother says "no," Carrie gets upset, cries, screams, kicks chairs and tries to hit her mother. So Mom uses paradox. She says to Carrie:

"You have so much anger inside of you right now, I want you to get it all out. So, Carrie, I want you to sit on this kitchen chair and for the next 10 minutes I want you to scream and holler as loud as you can. I insist that you do this so you get all your anger out."

Again, if Carrie refuses to do it, then she learns that she can stop her tantrum behavior any time she wants. She learns that she's in charge of her emotions—which, by the way, is a great lesson for any child to learn. If Carrie yells and screams she cooperates with her mother's order. In fact, when this paradox is presented to a child, and the child does what the parent demands, the behavior doesn't last the entire 10 or 15 minutes. The child starts yelling and screaming while Mom or Dad goes about business in the kitchen, and then quits because no one's paying attention and because it's actually hard to yell for 10 or 15 minutes. Again, when the child stops yelling after five minutes, he or she experiences control over the tantrum behavior.

Before this paradoxical experience, Carrie felt out of control with tantrums. She felt she couldn't stop herself from having tantrums. In using paradox, the parents teach her through her own experience that she *does* have control. She can decide to have a tantrum or not, and she can stop at any time during the tantrum. This is a wonderful lesson for a child to experience.

Finally, paradox works well when your child can't take "no" for an answer and continually negotiates until he gets a "yes." Twelve-year-old David wants to go to the shopping mall on Saturday afternoon with a couple of his friends. You tell him "no" and state your reasons why. He doesn't accept your answer and begins the debating and negotiating process.

If this negotiating ends up in a fight between the two of you, then break out of it by using paradox. Try to unhook from the conflict by saying:

"David, you and I are having trouble talking with each other. You seem to have so many reasons and arguments inside of you that I want you to sit down here and write out every reason you can think of as to why you should go to the mall. Write them out in detail. Take at least 15 minutes to do so."

Often children won't want to sit and write. But telling them to do so stops the verbal negotiating that only catches the emotions of you and your child. It breaks the arguing pattern and forces the child to:

1. either quit negotiating by doing the writing, or
2. not do the writing and accept your decision that he can't go the mall.

Telling David to write down his arguments changes the negotiating dynamic. As a result, he may give up his negativity and accept your "no," or he may write out all his arguments and still want you to say "yes."

If his arguments aren't persuasive, you say to him:

"David, I appreciate how you're thinking about this, but the answer is still 'no.' And the discussion is over." Then walk away and keep quiet.

Thinking paradoxically helps you break up patterns with your child that aren't working. It adds a different twist to the regular routines you run with your child, and it frees your child to begin responding in new and more positive ways.

Principle 22

At times, when the new, appropriate behavior appears, predict a relapse.

You need to be careful about this principle. Sometimes you use it and other times you don't. What I mean is this: Carrie decides not to yell and scream while sitting on the kitchen chair. You say: "Carrie, I really want you to do this, because it seems it's very important for you to yell when I say 'no.'" When she insists on not yelling, you say: "Well, okay. But I don't think you're going to be able to keep from yelling the next time I have to say 'no' to you for something. I'm pretty sure you'll just have another screaming fit."

That's predicting the relapse. Obviously, what you're doing is challenging the oppositional child. By telling her she will return to her yelling behavior, you hope she will oppose you by not doing so.

Decide to use this fourth step only if you think the challenge will work with your child. I wouldn't use it if the child feels very inadequate about herself, because then your prediction of a relapse could become a self-fulfilling prophesy. Use it if your child rises to challenges. Don't overstate it and don't berate the child. Simply predict that the child's behavior will be hard to change. And you don't expect that it will change.

Principle 23

Choose carefully the areas in which you use paradox.

Use paradox only after all other approaches have failed. And use it only when you sense your child is being oppositional. In other words, when you see your son benefitting in some way from opposing you, then paradox is an effective strategy to use.

At times, parents feel that paradox is manipulative and "gamey." I suppose it is, in a way. But so is oppositional behavior. Sometimes you have to enter the game in order to break up the game. If you keep trying to resist a behavior and your resistance is precisely the reinforcement your child craves, then you keep the system alive.

Paradox is a way of significantly changing the system and breaking into the oppositional behavior of your child.

Paradox works best with younger children. Teens don't respond well to paradox, as I've indicated. Nor do teen issues fit a paradoxical approach well. For instance, you don't use paradox when your child is threatening suicide. You don't use it when she is drinking alcohol or using drugs. You don't employ it when you discover he's having sex with his girlfriend. In these situations you don't say: "I insist that you do more of this behavior."

Be choosy about using paradox. It seems to work best with behaviors that are repetitious and are not destructive of the child or someone else. I think it works best with temper tantrums, swearing, messy rooms, constant negotiating, eating habits at the table, and simple things like that.

Principle 24

In disciplining children, use paradox as your last approach.

There is an order to follow in dealing with children around misbehavior. I mentioned it earlier, but want to highlight it again. Work with your children in this order:

1. Talk with your child, asking for change and helping him or her see the purpose of the change.
2. If that doesn't work, use your authority, and use it as long as it works.
3. If that doesn't work, change the system of your interaction with your child. Look to change *you* rather than change your child. Your change will bring about change in your child.
4. If that doesn't work, use the logical consequences approach, giving your child freedom to misbehave, giving him or her choices and establishing and enforcing the consequences of those choices.
5. Finally, in cases of oppositional children, if none of the above works, then use paradox when it's appropriate.

Chapter 5

Important General
Discipline Issues

There are a couple of principles in disciplining that cut across all the approaches to teaching children how to become more responsible. In this last chapter I want to explore those principles.

Principle 25

**Children need structure and discipline
in their lives.**

Sometimes people think I'm soft on discipline, especially when I talk about getting out of power struggles with children.

"Just get tough," they say. "Don't give in to them."

Recently I was counseling a mother and father on ways of dealing with their obstinate and rebellious teenager. I said, "When you get into the big fights, that's the time for you to back out. If a particular issue of conflict destroys the relationship it isn't worth fighting about."

The father almost died of shock when I said that. "No way," he countered. "I'm the father and Jim will obey."

He thought that was tough discipline. I call that stupid discipline. Increasing the force doesn't work. Furthermore, it models for the child the loss of control and discipline that is operating in the parent's own life.

Parents who blast away at their children and keep upping the ante as the children resist demonstrate their own undisciplined behavior. No wonder their children are acting out of control.

I believe the approaches I've shared with you in this book reflect solid structure and present accurate, clear boundaries for children. If you keep your head, and as calmly as possible go about your job of teaching your children how to act responsibly, you will notice how disciplined and structured you actually are. And your children will benefit from that structure.

Putting structure in your children's lives means

setting clear boundaries for them and then sticking with those boundaries. Young children have no boundaries. This isn't something they're born with. They have to learn how far they can go.

For the first seven months of life you needn't worry about setting limits for your children. They can't really push into areas that are dangerous for them. About the most annoying thing they can do is to keep on crying when they want something or to awaken frequently throughout the night.

But from seven months—the creeping stage—on through high school, your children test the limits of your and society's structures. Your job as a parent is to help them learn just how far they can go without hurting themselves or others. Your job is to draw the lines in the sand and say to them: "This is as far as you can go."

By putting structure in the lives of your children, you not only teach them how to act responsibly in our world, but you also help them better define themselves.

Young children easily spill beyond their own boundaries. They invade your space and time. They interfere in their brothers' and sisters' affairs. They get in the way because they don't know where they end and someone else begins.

Structure and boundaries help them learn who they are by learning where they stop and where others start.

Principle 26

Being consistent is the most important aspect of discipline.

More than anything else, consistency drives discipline. It's the backbone of any approach to putting structure in your children's lives. And it's not easy.

After setting a limit or imposing a consequence, you often have second thoughts and feelings. You wonder if you're being too harsh. You feel bad about denying your child something. You see the sadness in his big, brown eyes. Then you think, "Oh well, maybe this one time I'll let it go."

No. Don't succumb to the temptation. The tears will dry from those cocker spaniel eyes. Stick with your decisions. Don't change your mind.

The only exception to changing your mind is when the consequence is obviously too severe for the crime. That usually occurs when you react emotionally and quickly to something your child has done. If you say "You're grounded for the rest of the summer," you need to change your mind about that.

Other typical parental responses that can be changed—and should be changed—include:

- "No TV for a month."
- "You have to pay for breaking that chair"

(yelled at an eight-year-old).

- "I'm selling your Nintendo game tomorrow."
- "You stay in your room the rest of the day" (said at 10:00 AM).
- "Don't ever ask to go to McDonald's again because it's not going to happen."
- "You will not drive the car for the rest of the summer" (announced on June 1st).

Those impassioned threats need to be changed. But the majority of consequences you set should stay in force. Changing your mind teaches children that limits don't really mean limits, and "If I work at it hard enough, I can change Mom's mind." Then you get the double-barreled negotiating tactic.

Once you set a limit, stick to it. This is where you need to be emotionally tough. If you can't stand to see your child sad and pathetic, then look away. Don't get drawn into any negotiating with your child. Once you have determined an appropriate consequence, hold the line.

If three weeks later your consequence isn't getting the desired behavior, add to it. Usually you don't want to remove the consequence, unless it's clear that it's not having its desired effect. But give yourself three weeks, as a rule of thumb, before you change it.

Consistency itself is a boundary. When your child knows you aren't changing your mind, he or she usually complies. Your child will fight you and negotiate only if he or she knows you can't hold your position. So hang tough! Don't waffle. Stay focused.

Principle 27

In a two-parent family, make sure you work together in disciplining your children.

When parents bring me a child with behavioral problems, I want to know how the parents get along with each other. More often than not, their relationship is conflicted, or they have very different views on how to discipline their child. Once they clear up their own relationship or can agree on how to discipline their child, the child's "misbehavior" gradually disappears.

When one parent is strict and the other is lenient, the child feels confused and ambivalent. Such a state creates anxiety, which needs to get resolved. So the child makes a decision to behave in a certain way, which may please one of the parents and displease the other, or may displease both parents. The child can't win.

The result is no one is happy and the tension and anxiety continue.

Tina wants to go to bed later than nine o'clock, her mother's determined time. Her dad doesn't mind if she stays up later. Every Tuesday Mom has a class in the evening and doesn't get home until 10:00 PM. With Mom gone, Dad lets Tina stay up until 9:45 PM and then hussles her to bed "before your mother gets home."

You can see what happens here. Tina and Dad become aligned with one another against Mom. Tina learns to go to Dad whenever she wants something. Even if she has to ask Mom, she knows she has a court of appeals in her father. If Mom says "no," she goes to Dad for a second, more favorable opinion.

Dad and Mom need to come together on issues of parenting and discipline. Dealing with a child in the same way gives her consistency and predictability. It allows those important boundaries to get well-established.

When the parents are inconsistent due to their philosophical differences on disciplining, they help their child maintain a state of confusion about her boundaries. That causes anxiety in the child, which leads to more acting out behavior.

But what do you do if you and your parenting partner disagree on issues involving discipline? Usually the disagreements center around one being seen as too strict and the other seen as being too lenient. If, through discussion, you cannot resolve your differences, then I strongly urge you to lean in the direction of the more lenient parent. The stricter parent often borders on being rigid in his or her style of discipline. When a parent gets too rigid, he or she tends to focus on every piece of behavior emitted from the child. The rigid parent wants a lot of control in the child's life. He or she seeks to think for the child, act for him and decide for him. The child never gets the opportunity to think for himself, make his own choices and his own mistakes.

Furthermore, the rigid parent tends to get angry easily because he or she has so many rules. When the child breaks these rules the parent becomes upset. The more rules he or she has, the more opportunity for them to be broken, leading to more chances for anger.

The child who lives with an angry parent carries considerable fear and anxiety. He also learns how to *avoid* the parent's wrath. One excellent way to avoid a parent is to lie to him or her. Thus the rigid parent induces fear in the child, which keeps the child distant from the parent by lying and living a secret life.

The parent who is more flexible and lenient has a better chance at staying connected to the child as he grows up.

Being lenient (I like the word *flexible* better) doesn't mean unstructured. A flexible parent can hold firm to the rules that have been established. But he or she won't see every issue as a major factor in the child's life. A flexible parent lets go of the "small stuff." The rigid parent thinks everything is big and has to be attacked quickly and with force.

I suggest that rigid parents lighten up. Relax a little and choose carefully the issues in which you want to draw a line in the sand. Preferably, two parents can agree on how to discipline, but if you can't, please go with the parent who is more flexible.

Principle 28

Be careful not to give your children too much of everything.

A number of years ago, while flying Piedmont Airlines, I pulled a copy of their monthly magazine from the chair pouch in front of me. As I paged through it I came across an article by Dr. Bruce Baldwin. The title caught my attention—"The Cornucopia Kids: Giving Children Too Much May Be Giving Too Little" (*Piedmont Airlines Magazine,* May 1985).

Cornucopia kids are the children who have too much. They get whatever they want. They think the world owes them. They're entitled. When someone says "no," they can't cope. Most important, cornucopia kids have not made the connection between *effort* and *reward*. They don't think that effort leads to reward. Instead, they believe they ought to be rewarded just for gracing the earth with their presence. Consequently, they don't work for their privileges and rewards.

These kids often have high aspirations and fantastic dreams, but they don't have the discipline (there's that word again in a different context) to stay with a project. I can't tell you how many kids I have known over the years who have told me they want to become a professional basketball or baseball player, a rock musician, an actress or a physician, but they don't work toward it.

Cindy wanted to be a stand-out basketball player in high school so she could get a scholarship to play college ball. I told her if that's what she wanted, she had to put herself on a schedule (discipline and structure) and practice every day. She made chart after chart of drills to do—dribbling, shooting, foot-speed, conditioning. Her commitments lasted about two or three days. Then it got hard and she quit. She didn't know the lesson: effort begets reward.

That's why children need discipline in their lives. They can't have it too easy. They need to learn how to put limits in their own lives by having limits placed on them by their parents. The limits you place need not be rigid and super-demanding. They need to be reasonable and very consistent.

According to Dr. Baldwin, cornucopia kids tend to demand only the best, engaging in self-indulgence and excessive behavior. They show a contempt for material things, even though they have great wants in this area. They show a high need for constant stimulation and have difficulty sticking to tasks and completing projects or achieving goals. These children often lack compassion for others and are willing to lie in order to get what they want. It's not a pretty picture that Dr. Baldwin paints.

Many of these characteristics are a direct result of a lack of discipline in the children's lives. Discipline helps children develop internal motivation, which is essential for living responsibly and effectively in our world. Dr. Baldwin offers some suggestions for helping children develop internal drive. Here they are:

1. Give your child regular work responsibilities.
2. Refrain from giving your child too many "freebies."
3. Limit television viewing time.
4. Try teaching your child to be sensitive to others.
5. Insist that your child complete his or her tasks.
6. Help your child cope with failure.
7. Stress personal values over conformity to other people.
8. Insist that your child be accountable.
9. Create cooperative projects for your child to experience.
10. Set clear boundaries for work.

You don't want to indulge your children. I know you love them dearly, but love them with boundaries around their behavior. Love them unconditionally, but realize you have a major job to perform in their regard. You need to help them live responsibly in this world. They need to be clear about who they are and what works for their good and the good of others.

They gain that knowledge, in part, through your ability to discipline, set structures and boundaries in their lives and consistently help them experience the consequences of their behaviors.

Principle 29

You can change behavior through discipline, but you can't always change values through discipline.

One of the things you realize as your children grow up is that you can control your children's behavior only when they are in your presence. If you tell Ann not to watch television and you go to the store, Ann may well watch television. The controls in Ann's life are still external. She doesn't have a sense yet of respect for your desires and an ability to control her own desires when they run contrary to yours.

When disciplining and issuing commands to your children, realize you are acting on their *behaviors*, not necessarily their values. Of course, you hope that by altering their behaviors, they also see the value underneath and accept it. But you do not influence their values directly by disciplining them. You get yourself upset if you expect children's values to change because of your discipline.

With discipline, focus only on changing behavior. Values change and develop more indirectly, through modeling, storytelling, showing examples and so on. You can't force children to change their values.

For example, you can force your daughter to go to church with you, but you can't make her pray while she's there. You might be able to make her say the words of prayer, but you can't make her appreciate it or share your beliefs about it.

Here are some of the value issues that discipline cannot directly control:

1. Friends: You can insist that your child not hang around with another person, but you can't stop her from liking that person. And you control their being together only as long as your daughter is in your presence.

2. Alcohol and drugs: You can make rules about no drinking or not taking drugs in your home—or anywhere else—but you can enforce such a rule only when you're there. And your rule won't necessarily influence your child's values about those chemicals.

3. Sex: The rule "no sex" for a preteen or teenager sounds like a good rule to you as a parent, but you influence the values about sexuality more by your own beliefs and behaviors than by making rules.

4. School work: While you can use disciplinary approaches to make sure your son is doing his homework, your discipline doesn't mean he will now value studying. Again, the value comes in your own appreciation of studying. One simple way you can show this to your child is by turning off the television and getting involved in your own reading or studying.

5. Respect for others: You can discipline your child for taking his sister's compact discs, but you teach respect by showing respect for all people.

Discipline influences and controls behavior. It doesn't always influence your children's values.

Of course, you hope that through your discipline, your children will value themselves and others more, but I wouldn't focus on the value aspect of discipline. In other words, pay attention to controlling and modifying your children's *behavior* through discipline. And remember that what your children value is affected more by your modeling and the presentation of your beliefs and concerns than by the practice of discipline.

Conclusion

Disciplining your child is the most difficult aspect of parenting. It demands a balance between firmness and leniency. It calls for wisdom and judgment no less than that needed by Solomon. It's enveloped in a range of feelings from anger to tenderness. It summons every psychological skill available to you.

Disciplining your child is not something you like doing as a parent. It means your child is testing the boundaries and getting into trouble. Your job is to step in and help him or her experience the limits and the consequences of his or her behavior.

To discipline well, you need to be a very *conscious* parent. That is, you need to be aware, always thinking, always observing your child and yourself. When you are aware of what's going on, you have *choices* about how to respond. If you're not aware, you respond automatically. And automatic responses under stress are more often too strong and dramatic.

I hope that this book helps you stay aware and realize you have a variety of ways to respond to your child's misbehavior. To increase your awareness and vigilance, talk about the principles identified here with a friend or your parenting partner. Sharing thoughts and feelings about your parenting reinforces these principles and keeps you conscious of what you're doing and what options you have in any situation.

Finally, please realize that any effort you make in disciplining your child is for the sake of teaching him or her how to live more responsibly in the world. That's the silver lining in the dark cloud that can hover over the difficult job of setting limits in your child's life and helping your child experience the consequences of his or her behavior.

Review of the Principles of Discipline

1. Use verbal authority as long as it works.

2. With young children, just say "no" and stick to it.

3. Keep lectures to a bare minimum. Nobody listens beyond the first sentence anyway.

4. On some issues you may have to make requests forever.

5. When you have a need, tell your child about it and request his or her help. But don't use discipline to get *your* need met.

6. To break the patterns that don't work, look first to change your behavior as parents.

7. Once you make a change in your behavior, stick with it no matter how awful your child's behavior gets.

8. Realize that when a child misbehaves regularly, there is a problem in the family system.

9. If your responses to your child don't work, then change your responses. Don't keep doing more of the same.

10. Your child's misbehavior yields positive rewards for him or her. Know what your child gets from misbehaving.

11. To change a family system, first try to change your own behavior.

12. Think in terms of discipline through logical consequences rather than through punishment.

13. Give your child the freedom to behave improperly as well as to behave properly.

14. Perform each step of the discipline process consistently.

15. Consequences must flow directly out of the child's misbehavior and cause hardship for your child.

16. Stick to your consequences once you set them.

17. Be selective about when to use consequences with your children. Don't overdo it.

18. Create a double bind situation for your child.

19. Go *with* your child's behavior instead of against it.

20. Reframe and respect the experience of your child.

21. Command the behavior you wish to stop.

22. At times, when the new, appropriate behavior appears, predict a relapse.

23. Choose carefully the areas in which you use paradox.

24. In disciplining children, use paradox as your last approach.

25. Children need structure and discipline in their lives.

26. Being consistent is the most important aspect of discipline.

27. In a two-parent family, make sure you work together in disciplining your children.

28. Be careful not to give your children too much of everything.

29. You can change behavior through discipline, but you can't always change values through discipline.

About the Author

Dale R. Olen, Ph.D., lives in Germantown, Wisconsin, with his wife, Joelyn, and their two children, Andy and Amy. Andy studies political science in college; Amy studies, works, and plays basketball in high school. They have a friendly beagle and an independent cat.

Dale received his doctorate in psychology from the University of Kansas in 1973. A year earlier he founded **The Justice and Peace Center** in Milwaukee, a social action organization attempting to create structural and societal change. During this time he realized that justice meant creating the opportunity for people to exercise their most basic right; namely, the right to live humanly. In his effort to understand what "living humanly" meant, he identified 14 "life skills" that fully alive people exhibit. He realized that his life's work was to help people develop these life skills so they could live full and happy lives. As a result, he started **Life Skills Center**, a mental health agency that he still directs today.

Dale teaches life skills through his writing, his lectures and workshops, and by doing psychotherapy. Since most people spend the majority of their time and energy at home and in work, he has concentrated his teaching in those two areas. He directs his life skills programs and materials toward families and businesses.

Dr. Olen is available for lectures and workshops on parenting and marriage, and he offers training programs for businesses. To invite Dr. Olen to speak with your group or to conduct a workshop, please call JODA Communications at 414-475-1600.

Index

Life Skills Parenting Series

FALL 1994 PUBLICATION:

Parenting for the First Time

Packed with tips, cautions and wisdom for the new parent.

Like Dale Olen's other books, this one gives you specific principles and tools needed for the journey about to begin. Dale writes about the range and depth of emotions you experience as a new parent. He explains your reactions to a new child in the home. He offers suggestions on patterns of behavior to initiate from day one.

Here's your guide as you take on the awesome responsibility of bringing a human being into this world. Or, if you're already a dad or mom, this book makes a great gift for that family member or friend who's about to become a new-born parent.

SPRING 1995 PUBLICATION:

Teaching Children to Like Themselves

Here's the book that answers the concern of almost every parent: "How can I help my child feel better about him or herself?"

In this easy-to-read book, Dale Olen reveals the causes of high and low self-esteem. He shows how children develop their sense of self and the role you play in that process. Then he describes the actions you need to take and the attitudes you can impart to your children to raise their self-images.

Through the pages of this book you sense the sacred core of your child's life. And you have the means to caress that life and give it growth.

continued

Life Skills Parenting Series, *continued*

FALL 1995 PUBLICATION:

How to Parent Your Teenager

To do this job right demands a revolution in your mind and actions. The ways you parented when your child was small no longer apply. Now you need to respond and act in more thoughtful, calm and careful ways.

In this exciting and insightful book, Dale leads you through the conversion you must go through to handle the issues and energies of your teen. He describes in detail how to talk with your teenager and tells you exactly what to say and how to say it.

Filled with dialogues between parents and teens, this book is necessary reading to help you and your teenager enjoy these vital years.

JODA Communications, Ltd.
10125 West North Avenue
Milwaukee, WI 53226
Telephone: 414-475-1600

The next two pages contain ordering
information

The Life Skills Series by Dale R. Olen, Ph.D.

Quantity	Title	Unit Price	Total
	Accepting Yourself: Liking Yourself All of the Time (005-9)	$5.95	
	Thinking Reasonably: Reaching Emotional Peace Through Mental Toughness (004-0)	$5.95	
	Meeting Life Head On: Moving into Life with Courage—Not Backing Away in Fear (006-7)	$5.95	
	Managing Stress: Learning to Pace Your Chase Through Life (003-2)	$5.95	
	Communicating: Speaking and Listening to End Misunderstanding and Promote Friendship (007-5)	$5.95	
	Being Intimate: Achieving Union With Others Without Losing Yourself (008-3)	$5.95	
	Reducing Anger: Harnessing Passion and Fury to Work for You—Not Against Others (009-1)	$5.95	
	Overcoming Fear: Reaching for Your Dreams and Knowing Peace of Mind (010-5)	$5.95	
	Defeating Depression: Lifting Yourself from Sadness into Joy (011-3)	$5.95	
	Resolving Conflict: Learning How You Both Can Win and Keep Your Relationship (012-1)	$5.95	
	10-book set of above titles	$49.95	

TOTAL ORDER

Shipping and handling: For 1-2 books, add $1.50;
for 3-6 books, add $3.50; for 7-10 books, add $4.50

If Wisconsin resident, add 5% or 5 1/2% sales tax

TOTAL $

METHOD of PAYMENT

☐ Check enclosed. (Make checks payable to JODA Communications, Ltd.)

☐ VISA   ☐ MASTERCARD

Credit Card No. _____ Expiration Date _____

Signature _____

Mail order form along with payment to: **JODA Communications, Ltd.**
10125 West North Avenue, Milwaukee WI 53226

Or you may call **1-414-475-1600.** Please have your VISA or MASTERCARD information ready.

Please send books to:

	Name
	Street Address
City	State	Zip Code
	Phone

ORDER FORM

THE THOUGHTFUL ART OF DISCIPLINE
TEACHING RESPONSIBILITY WHEN YOUR CHILD MISBEHAVES

QUANTITY	No. of COPIES	DISCOUNT	UNIT PRICE	TOTAL
	1-2		8.95	
	3-5	10%	8.06	
	6-10	15%	7.61	
	11-20	20%	7.16	
	over 20	25%	6.71	

Add shipping & handling: 1-2 books, $2.00;
3-5 books, $4.00; 6-10 books, $5.00.
For larger quantities, please call JODA for shipping costs

Wisconsin residents add $5\frac{1}{2}$% sales tax

TOTAL

METHOD of PAYMENT

☐ **Check enclosed. (Make payable to JODA Communications, Ltd.)**

☐ **VISA**   ☐ **MASTERCARD**

Credit Card No._____Expires_____

Signature_____

Please mail this order form with your payment to:

JODA Communications, Ltd.
10125 West North Avenue, Milwaukee, WI 53226

Or you may call **1-414-475-1600**. Please have your VISA or MASTERCARD
information ready.

Send books to: (PLEASE PRINT)

name
street address
city   state   zip code
phone